Lee's book has been an inspirati~~on~~ me ideas and a format to write m~~y~~ ~~g~~ ~~y~~ ~~my children,~~ grandchildren and future descendants. It is a blessing for all those looking for guidance and seeking inspiration. Words are inadequate to express my gratitude. Without your book, I would still be floundering, seeking ways to express myself, searching for something tangible to leave behind for my family. The written word, a legacy, a blessing. Thank you.

Violetta Strickland.

Thank you, Lee Miller for creating a magnificent way to get started with recording life memories. Not only did your book provide a guideline for helping me recall and preserve events in my life but also with my family structure. The guidebook has provided me the method and encouragement to create a written legacy for my children and grandchildren.

Amanda Barnes

Lee Miller's book, *The Journey: A Celebration of Life*, has provided me with a structure to begin writing my life story. It is an important tool in encouraging me to write and research both my family and personal history through developing a time line, using memory triggers and referring to specific sections on life experiences. In utilizing *The Journey*, I plan to leave a legacy for family members and close friends and to publish my memoirs. I want to share my life experiences and what I have learned with others as a means of empowerment. As a professional caregiver and hospice volunteer through her book, I will be able to assist my clients in writing an ethical will that they and family members will greatly benefit from as they share their values and lessons learned.

Donna Wylie

We would not dare have attempted to produce "A Glimpse Into the Life of Becca Dalton" without the assistance of Lee Miller and her guidebook. The organized and systematized approach to collecting materials and details enabled us to complete what first appeared as a nearly impossible feat.

Harry and Becca Dalton

The Journey
A Celebration of Life

Becky –

Enjoy the Journey and
celebrate your life!

Blessings

Jug miller
10-13-07

The Journey
A Celebration of Life

❧ *a guidebook for writing your life story* ❧

lee q. miller

TATE PUBLISHING & *Enterprises*

Published by Tate Publishing & Enterprises, LLC
127 E. Trade Center Terrace | Mustang, Oklahoma 73064 USA
1.888.361.9473 | www.tatepublishing.com

Tate Publishing is committed to excellence in the publishing industry. The company reflects the philosophy established by the founders, based on Psalms 68:11,
"The Lord gave the word and great was the company of those who published it."

Book design copyright © 2007 by Tate Publishing, LLC. All rights reserved.
Cover design by Chris Webb
Interior design by Janae J. Glass

Published in the United States of America

ISBN: 978-1-6024708-5-9
07.04.10

I dedicate this book to the memories of my sister, Susan; my father, Bill; and my mother, Flo, who taught me the importance of celebrating life.

Acknowledgements

A special thanks goes to my husband, Jerry, whose support, encouragement, unending patience, and love give meaning to my life and enable me to continue my journey of personal growth and self-discovery. His companionship along the roads we have traveled continues to make my journey more meaningful. I give to my children, Kimberly, Kathy, and Brad, a world of thanks for allowing me the opportunity to spend the time necessary to accomplish the completion of this book. Your assistance and suggestions in the entire process were invaluable. The four of you are what I celebrate most in my life.

To my siblings, Ab, Kay, and Ann and their spouses, thank you for your belief in me and for sharing the memories of Susan, Mom and Dad. To my cousin, Jane Wagner, goes a special thank you for her inspiration, motivation and continued support in so many facets of this undertaking.

My gratitude also goes to Dr. Tom Moore, Dean of the College of Arts and Sciences and to Dr. Dave Rankin, Director, Master of Liberal Arts Program at Winthrop University, for their inspiration, motivation, instruction and guidance. Additionally, a special thank you goes to Dr. Jonathan Marx and Dr. Jennifer Solomon for their years of mentoring, research collaboration and friendships, to Dr. Ameda Manetta for her endorsement of this book as a viable tool for social workers and gerontology professionals and to Dr. Hal Caldwell for his eloquent foreword.

In your unique and specials ways, each of you has contributed to the completion of *The Journey: A Celebration of Life*. Without your assistance it would not have been possible. Thank you!

To my readers, I thank you for taking the time to celebrate life through this book. It is my wish that *The Journey: A Celebration of Life* will bring you and your loved ones many hours of joy, hope, encouragement and self-discovery as you prepare a legacy that will be cherished forever.

Foreword

Delving into oneself is never an easy task, but it is a task that, for most of us, needs to be done often. There are those who would say that such a task is essential for mental and emotional health and well-being. Although there are a multitude of reasons we may use to shirk the responsibility of focusing inward, the benefits of doing so are tremendous.

It is doubtful that one can ascertain his or her place in any social structure without honest introspection, but it is absolutely impossible to examine the structure and operation of society's most elemental group— the family—without involving an analysis of self. Lee Miller's work is designed to assist with the mechanics of gathering data to incorporate into a study of one's place in the family, although it goes far beyond the typical scope of genealogy. While genealogical research and study are invaluable in finding one's place in the family structure, these endeavors merely form the framework for a much larger entity, that of acknowledging and perpetuating beliefs and values. This multi-faceted approach sets Miller's work apart from a large body of literature in the field.

To relate the tasks of family research and analysis to a "journey" is not only appropriate, but it also establishes several principles that are inherent in such a task:

1. It is the passing of time that substantiates the validity of values in a family structure;
2. A journey has a beginning and a destination, although these points are limited by the technology of recording events and the initiative of individuals involved;
3. The preservation of family history and legends is eminently easier with a guided approach and useful tools; and
4. Communication is the key word when dealing with the identification and preservation of values and beliefs.

Because we deal with a myriad of individuals and situations, many of which are unique, it is imperative to have options when it comes to recording events which are part of any history. Thankfully, Ms. Miller's work addresses the use of numerous tools and approaches to gathering and preserving information. A seasoned family historian or genealogist relies on numerous tools and approaches designed for linking data. The lack of information about various techniques for recording information is often the stumbling block that terminates the work of beginners. Ms. Miller has included information that will be relevant to novice investigators as well as to experienced researchers.

Writing from a lifetime of experience, the author has chosen topics that are essential to a creditable family history. She addresses the importance of self-understanding as a prelude to making sense of data about others, the significance of documentation, the need for compassion in dealing with those who may be reluctant to share information, the joy of living, and the inevitability of death. Ample examples, some from the author's experience, illuminate the methodology of research and humanize the process of gathering data and relating individuals and family groups. The warmth of the author is as evident as her skill in linking individuals and extracting values from data.

Far too many individuals, writers included, perpetuate the belief that genealogy is a pursuit for the elderly. Although it is often true that one needs the perspective gained through years of living to find success and fulfillment in family research, the author advocates the "life review" process for younger adults. The passion of youth, while not a substitute for experience, can be a powerful force in the quest for personal growth.

A generous amount of space in this volume is given to the use of personal history in hospitals, nursing homes, and various social service agencies. The role of caregivers is dealt with sensitively and with compassion. Many examples are given to illustrate the need for closure to life among the elderly and dying; yet, the book does not become dark and morose.

It is noteworthy to examine the connection between life histories and ethical wills. One can exist without the other, but both are enhanced by the presence of the other. A life history is closely allied with genealogy, while an ethical will is the statement of an individual who wishes to transmit personal and family values to future generations. Although a merger of these two documents is not necessarily the best use of one's time and energy, the writing of each is enhanced by the insights gained from the other. The author makes convincing arguments to spend time in examining both the cognitive and affective aspects of both of these related genres of writing.

Of the many positive attributes of this book, two are outstanding in my mind. The first is the underlying principle that the process of the "journey" will lead to sharing with others. Like any memorable journey or other experience, it is richer when shared. When deep insights are not shared, the problem may be with the sensitivity of information; we simply do not want to become vulnerable by letting others peek inside our lives. More often, however, the thing that prohibits sharing is simply the lack of communication among family members. Far too often we limit the depth of family discussions to work, the weather, and the mechanics of daily living, rather than bearing our souls to those who should mean the most to us. The casual tone and gentle approach that Lee Miller has taken makes the gathering of information and the stating of beliefs and values almost incidental to the process. Communication with others is inherent, although some may unfortunately, deliver the message "from the grave." The richest experiences are those shared while all parties are alive and able to communicate and discuss things that are most precious to the one recording the journey.

The second most notable contribution of this volume is the sense of fulfillment that comes from completing a task before death. We need to approach the end of life with a sense of completion, a feeling of satisfaction, and a resolution of difficulties that we may have encountered during life. Our own lives will come to a peaceful end, and later generations will learn from us. They will learn family history; they will value the process of giving to others; they will find comfort in the love that we bequeath to future generations. As the author so beautifully stated, "What a priceless investment in forever."

Hal Caldwell, Ph.D.
Ethical Wills of Indiana

Table of Contents

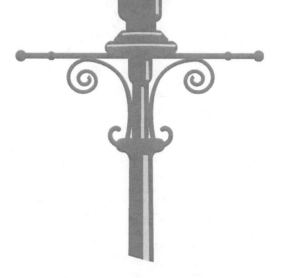

"Do not follow where the path may lead. Go instead where there is no path and leave a trail."
~ Ralph Waldo Emerson

Introduction

Life is a journey. Most of us spend our journey anxiously wondering where the next bend in the road will take us. We are so consumed with the future that we seldom take the opportunity to reflect on the life experiences that link the past with the present. *The Journey: A Celebration of Life* is a guide to assist you in writing your life review.

The Journey: A Celebration of Life is an experience for people of all ages who are seeking an opportunity to reflect upon the events of their lives as they seek personal growth through self-discovery. *The Journey* provides an enjoyable experience as you remember the past and recognize the people and events that have helped shape you into the person you are today. This book can help you to share your values, beliefs, ethics, and the lessons you gleaned from the successes and failures of your life's experiences. You will be able to share your wishes, dreams, and visions for the future, and prepare a priceless legacy that future generations will cherish.

With the guidebook, you can preserve family history and legends. It is an opportunity to create memoirs that can be published. As you link the past and the present, you have a greater understanding of life's transitions, and you may experience resolution to broken relationships, conflicts or fears. *The Journey* provides encouragement, hope, a sense of peace, comfort and healing, and the courage to accept one's inevitable mortality. *The Journey* helps you celebrate your life more completely.

The Journey: A Celebration of Life begins with a how-to section, followed with a section of the tools necessary to make the trip an enjoyable adventure. Incorporated within the text are suggestions for information to include in your notebook such as genealogies, scrapbook memorabilia, photographs, poems, quotations and inspirational meditations. Each of the sections provides you, the traveler, with questions that will encourage reminiscence of each stage of life. At the end is an opportunity to create an Ethical Will/Legacy Letter that reflects and summarizes your values and provides a written legacy of how you want to be remembered.

You may choose to take the journey alone or with a companion. You may want to involve the entire family. The choice is yours. Sharing the journey can help you tackle those difficult issues and stay committed to the task of completing the process.

Preserving your stories may be done with a combination of technologies: audio or visual recording, computer transcription, photocopying or scanning, handwriting, and scrapbooking. *The Journey* serves as an easy-to-follow guide for a beautiful reliving of these priceless memories.

Reflecting on your life can bring self-discovery. Telling your life story can provide your family and loved ones with a priceless legacy. Hopefully, the experience will bring you rewards and be valuable in helping you adapt to and more fully understand the transitions in your life. On your journey you will recall stories of love, happiness, pain and sorrow. Lessons learned and wisdom gained can be shared in such a way that future generations will benefit. The story of your life is important to those who love you. It will be valued and treasured for many generations.

You are encouraged to write only what you are comfortable sharing. You can revisit any section at any time as you progress through your story and as you see how events have impacted your life. It is your story. Begin wherever you want. Share only what you desire. This book is simply a guide to aid you in the process.

Make sure you share the good as well as the bad, both the smooth and the rough roads of your journey. Someone else can learn valuable lessons from these memories. These experiences are meaningful because they have made you who you are today. You can also gain resolution or closure to events you thought had been resolved earlier. You may find yourself wanting to contact someone from the past so you can reminisce and share those special memories. You may feel that you need to contact one to mend a fence or right a wrong. There will be memories of people that you want to thank for their role in your life.

Take time to stop and write that note or make that phone call or visit. You won't regret it, and neither will they.

Each section provides you memory triggers in the form of questions to be answered. You may choose to answer all that are provided or only a few. There may be much more you want to share than is indicated by the questions. Everyone's life is unique, and your experiences should reflect that distinctiveness. I encourage you to go beyond the simple question that is provided. Go deeper within yourself and draw out the emotions and describe the events with all the senses coming alive, so when members of a distant generation pick up your book and begin to read, they will be transported back in time and will be able to see, feel, smell and experience in their minds exactly what you are describing.

Developing the concept of *The Journey: A Celebration of Life* began twelve years ago during the illness and death of my beloved sister, Susan. Susan lived for eight years with her illnesses, daily waging war against the enemies of breast and bone cancer. The last year of her life was spent putting the details of her life in order. She wanted to prepare her family and loved ones for her inevitable death. Many hours were spent by her bedside writing her funeral service and selecting poems, hymns, and scriptures to be shared at the service. She was specific about what she wanted people to remember about her. A list of her favorite things in life was included in the memorial booklet we compiled. She shared many precious memories as well as her legacy of values, hopes, dreams, inspirations, and her love for each person. This process of sharing seemed to bring great comfort to Susan and also to her family members. At some moments, it was hard to share and remember without tears. At other times we would be in hysterics as we remembered times past. There was time for Susan to share with her husband, children, and siblings one-on-one. These sacred sharings were just that—sacred, private, healing and comforting. The entire process of this sharing was a time of reconciliation for everyone.

A short three months after Susan's death, our family had to begin another grief process. My father died after being a patient for six months in a nursing home. He was in a place he did not want to be, with only a nurse to comfort him as he took those last breaths. During the last months of his life, he chose not to share what was facing him. He knew his time was limited, but he didn't want to burden anyone with his fears. He had accepted it. It was out of his hands. His wife and children had nothing to guide them in planning his funeral. Fortunately we had years of wonderful memories of him as a man, husband and father. These memories were compiled into a meaningful eulogy for his funeral. This process would have been so much easier if we had written it earlier during his lifetime. We could have truly shared the celebration of his life with him.

The contrast of the two deaths created tremendous conflict for me. It was seven years later when I was able to see another way to celebrate life and to approach death and dying with a loved one. My mother had been given a second chance at life. She had survived a close call with death and now was rallying to embrace what time she had remaining. It was during those last months that we began to write her life story. During the life review, Mom shared with me her childhood, marriage, parenting, widowhood and her hopes and dreams for her children, grandchildren and great grandchildren. She was able to put into writing the lessons she had learned in life, and she shared the wisdom gleaned from those lessons. She wanted to make sure that future generations would benefit from her life. Mother was able to express some of the disappointments in her life and to face those with resolution. We had completed a major portion of the book when she unexpectedly became ill and died three weeks later. She had had time to make peace with herself, others and God. Mom was ready to die. Her children and loved ones were able to let her go peacefully. As we surrounded her deathbed, holding hands and praying, she slowly but peacefully slipped away. We will all cherish the written legacy she left us.

Having seen the difference it made for individuals to conduct a life review and to share it with others before death reinforced my belief that an avenue to conduct these life reviews needed to be created. Thus the creation of *The Journey: A Celebration of Life* began.

While working on my Master of Liberal Arts degree at Winthrop University, I focused my studies in the areas of gerontology and sociology. For my final project I wanted to create a guidebook that could easily be handled by a senior citizen. I wanted family members to take the book with them when they visited their elders. The guidebook would be the perfect tool to stimulate conversations with their loved ones. It could serve as a guide to tape record the reminiscence sessions. I needed an easy-to-use guidebook for my life review workshops and training of volunteers and caregiver professionals. Another purpose was to create that "perfect gift" for the person who has everything. I wanted a tool that could be used in every type of counseling from addiction recovery, bereavement, anticipatory grief to ethical wills and legacy letters.

Research continues regarding the importance and relevance of life review in the dying process. Much more needs to be done. Anticipatory grief concerns professionals from the medical, social work, counseling and clergy fields, and caregivers, family members, and patients can all benefit from a greater understanding of what a person who is dying experiences. In the March 2001 issue of *American Family Physician,* anticipatory grief is defined as "the type of grief that people who are dying go through. Individuals feel this grief as they go through the physical and emotional changes that are part of the dying process." The article describes the phases, reinforcing that the phases will not occur in any certain order. "People can skip phases or even be in more than one phase at a time. The phases are shock, chaos, introspection, re-adaptation, and restitution."

During these phases the individual questions and tries to balance the past with the future. "How can I make the most of the time I have left?" It is at these times—when they are trying to understand what is happening to them, why it is happening and what the future holds—that life review in the form of *The Journey* can help. It gives them the opportunity to reflect on their entire life. They hopefully have time to address goals that they want to meet before they die. It provides the opportunity to touch base with the past, to reconcile differences, and to embrace friendships and special relationships. It can give them a pathway through the depression that accompanies the terminal illness process. *The Journey* can provide a legacy for future generations as they share what life has meant to them and what they have learned from their experiences.

John A. Kunz, in his article "Giving Voice to Lives: Reminiscence and Life Review" says, "Psychologist Erik Erikson's exploration of how an older adult reconciles with the inevitability of death is called integrity versus despair. Individuals gain wisdom from living long enough to reach a level of integrity about one's life. The older one becomes, the greater the awareness they have of the inevitability of death. At this time a natural reminiscence occurs. It is natural for them to want to share what they have learned to be true about their lives. They want to put their lives in perspective, resolve past conflicts, grieve losses and changes, forgive themselves and others, celebrate successes, and feel a sense of completion."

The Journey helps individuals to share these memories in a constructive and healing process.

Hospice agencies across the nation provide training for staff and volunteers in life review. If you wish to undergo training, I encourage you to contact your local hospice agency. Individuals facing death because of a terminal illness can benefit from the sharing that gives meaning and purpose to their lives. Healthcare institutions and professionals, clergy and social workers can assist in the life review and make it a positive experience. I have used the book to assist family members during bereavement if they were not able to capture the stories of their loved one before death. The section entitled Ethical Will/Legacy Letter is the perfect exercise and very easy to complete in a relatively short timeframe.

Lou Isbell, child and family development specialist, in her article, "*Living With Dying*" for a 1997 article in Human Environmental Sciences publication at Missouri University, provides great insight into living with dying. She mentions the shock and denial stage and how important it is to allow the individual to talk and to know that you are available to talk when he or she is ready. It is important to keep the lines of communication open.

There will be a point when denial turns to anger and the impact of the loss becomes real. It is during this time that *The Journey* may be of the greatest help in the resolution of this patient's acceptance of pending death. The process can help the individual to find a balance with the past and the future. It can help to make the most of what time is left. As the acceptance and understanding of the situation occur, *The Journey* will help the individual find new meaning for life and, hopefully, help handle the periods of depression. It will also help the individual create a priceless legacy for family and future generations. The transition to death will be more peaceful. Through the pages of *The Journey,* the family members will be able to visit their loved one and reminisce for many years. The grief and mourning process will be easier because the individual took the time to share what life meant to him or her. The wisdom shared will be handed down to future heirs. What a wonderful gift! What a priceless investment in forever!

This guidebook is for anyone seeking an avenue to personal growth and self-discovery, seeking emotional healing, seeking a deeper understanding and acceptance of life's transitions, coping with bereavement issues or seeking guidance in writing an ethical will. Due to the intensity of emotions that surface when one is seeking a deeper understanding and acceptance of life's transitions, you may find the process to be extremely emotional. If you have difficulty coping with the issues that surface, I encourage you to seek professional counseling.

Other areas where the book has been enjoyable and beneficial were in assisted living facilities as roundtable discussions or on individual basis. I have used the guidebook to facilitate memory therapy sessions for early on-set Alzheimer's patients, helping senior citizens to write their life story, and assisting in writing memoirs for publication. During my reminiscence sessions at local facilities, the residents were receptive and anxious to participate. The questions we discussed each Saturday morning gave them a bond with the other participants and provided topics for conversation during the week. The memories shared often brought peals of laughter, and sometimes tears were shed. Some participants struggled with recalling particulars about an event. With encouragement, they continued, and it seemed to generate additional memories that they couldn't wait to share. *The Journey: A Celebration of Life* can help train caregivers in these facilities to conduct life review sessions daily or weekly.

The process can also be a wonderful activity for family members and residents when they have their visits. I have been working on a collection of stories for an eighty-five-year-old gentleman. His son says the process is what is keeping him alive. Everyday he is organizing his memorabilia and jotting down stories to be told. The anticipation of our sessions gives him something to anticipate.

Younger adults want to begin the life review process for personal growth. Karen Martin said that the guidebook came about at the right time in her life. She wanted to return to journaling and to have an earnest venue for her writing, without filling up a bunch of pages with lots of temporary whinnying. "This book provided not only the motivation but also the template to guide my entries, to help my writing take on an added value."

Social Work professional and educator, Dr. Ametta Manetta, Ph.D., MSW, BSW, BA, LCSW and Assistant Professor at Winthrop University in the Department of Social Work, shares the importance of life review in the social work arena.

> For the last several years in American Society, aging has become medicalized, and death has become a taboo subject. As we begin the 21st century, social workers are turning back to a time when both were accepted as a normal part of life. In our efforts to help people accept death, we are focusing on helping them accept their life. One way of learning how to accept the life one has lived is by engaging in a review of one's own life. People who engage in life review are given the opportunity to relive the wonderful events and bring closure to the disappointing events by engaging in conversation about these events with another person.
>
> Life review can also be used with adults as they age and find

they are less able to care for themselves. As physical ability declines, some individuals begin to feel their use to society is depleted. Documenting their lives through the life review process provides a legacy of information and wisdom for the next generation. In turn, the personal narratives help older adults become comfortable and gain a deeper understanding and appreciation for the journey they have taken from birth to the final years of their lives.

The book can serve as a training tool for hospice caregivers, social workers, clergy, counselors and therapists. Educators and historians (oral and written) can benefit from the outlines and easy-to-follow sections of the book. As an expectant grandparent, I look forward to working with my husband, my daughter and her husband to prepare a legacy for our future grandchild. The book is for anyone seeking a meaningful way to celebrate life. No matter your age or stage of life, your stories are invaluable to those who know and love you today and for the future generations who will someday wonder about you and the time of life you lived, what you experienced and how you handled those experiences. We need the stories to keep us connected, to inspire and to cherish forever. The reasons to complete *The Journey: A Celebration of Life* are endless.

"To sit alone in the lamplight with a book spread out before you and hold intimate conversation with those of unseen generations such is a pleasure beyond compare."

~ Kenko Yoshida, Japanese essayist and poet (1283-1352)

How To Begin

1. Read the book to determine where you want to begin. You might want to be sequential and start at the beginning, or you may be at a point in your life where you want to begin in the Reflections sections and create your Ethical Will/Legacy Letter. The choice of where to start is yours.

2. Make a commitment to a specific time each day or week that you will travel on your journey of life review.

3. Find a comfortable place to sit and conduct your life review (a special chair, room or outside sanctuary) that allows you the space you need for reflection and review. If you are having someone accompany you on your journey, make sure they will also be comfortable.

4. Have something to hold all your materials and make sure it has room for expansion.

5. Atmosphere: You may want to have music playing in the background or a candle burning.

Tools

1. The Journey: A Celebration of Life.
2. Paper.
3. Comfortable pens or pencils.
4. File folders or large envelopes to organize pictures, memorabilia and notes.
5. Index cards (memory cards). You will want these handy so that as a memory occurs you can write it on the card and place it in an appropriate folder to respond to at a later time.
6. Storage bins or boxes to hold memorabilia, photographs, memory cards, envelops, and file folders.
7. A binder to hold your writings. Later you may opt to have it professionally bound.
8. Tape recorder, video camera, batteries, tapes.
9. If you decide to scan pictures there are printing shops that can scan these for you and you can incorporate them into your completed book, or you may scan the pictures yourself on your computer and print as you wish.
10. Transcriber (optional).
11. Computer (optional).

You will want to keep these materials easily accessible. Don't hide them. You will not want to take the time or trouble to put them up and pull them out every time you sit down to work. If you hide them, you will be tempted to delay the review. Stay faithful to the process.

"How far you go in life depends on your being tender with the young, compassionate with the aged, sympathetic with the striving and tolerant of the weak and strong, because someday in your life you will have been all of these."
~ Annon

Timeline

The Journey begins with creating a timeline that is divided into decades (mile markers). Each decade (mile marker) brings with it significant events in your life. As you remember these events, you will do so from your unique perspective. You will want to share these events and how they have helped to form your philosophy of life.

The first tick mark represents your date of birth to 10 years. The second tick mark represents the next 10 years and so on till you reach your current age.

Write pertinent information beside each tick mark, or just write birth date, events surrounding your birth, names of parents, siblings, and stories told about you as a child. Continue with your earliest memory, names of playmates, schools, teachers, classmates, and special events.

To create your timeline, use an unlined piece of paper, turned sideways (landscape). Draw a straight line and place tick marks for each decade. You may have several pages! As you label each decade, memories, names, and events will come to mind. Jot a single word or name down and expand on it later.

You may simply want to use a separate piece of paper for each decade.

"Knowing our past, we shall find strength
and wisdom to meet the present."
~ Gertrude Weil

Floor Plan

Another tool to help you pinpoint those memories is to draw a floor plan of your childhood home, or the home where you have lived the longest, or your favorite home. Just a rough sketch will do. As you enter each room, memories will come flooding back. Jot down one word or phrase that you can refer to later as you write the stories.

EXAMPLE: House Floor Plan

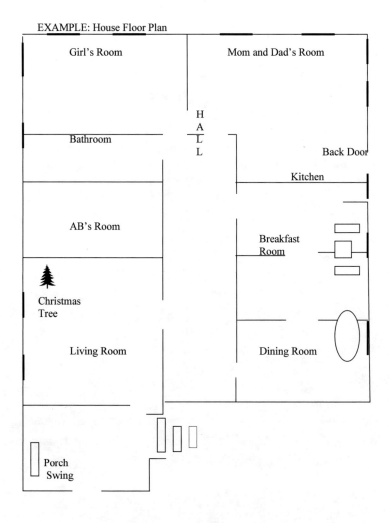

"No matter where you go; there you are."
~Buckaroo Banzai

"Leave a roadmap for the next generation.
Life is a work of art, designed by the one who lives it."
~Anon

Life Map

This may be a map of the United States or foreign countries where you may have lived. As you remember all the places you have lived—towns, and states—write the relevant dates or ages, number them and then write specific memory joggers for those locations.

You may have never lived but in one location. If this is the case, you might want to draw a map of the town, pinpoint your neighborhood, and place specific sites that have special significance for you. Indicate locations of the school buildings, local businesses, houses, and neighborhoods where you lived. Plot the places you worked. Remember to note the names of people.

You may want to use the map as an event map. Draw symbols or sketches depicting special events and dates you want to remember. You might want to depict the special milestones in your life. What you depict is up to you.

You might want to combine maps. These maps are spectacular when done in colored pencils or watercolors and then framed. They are a wonderful way to generate conversations as people view the interesting maps of your lifetime.

"Those who do not look upon
themselves as a link connecting the past with the
future do not perform their duty to the world."
~ Daniel Webster

Suggestions

Separating sections in the book will help you to group your life experiences. Remember, you are unique. Your life experiences will be different from others. Some of the sections will apply to you. Others will have no meaning whatsoever. Although you might not have served in the military, you may have been touched by war. The Military section is where you can share. You may never have been married nor had children; yet, you may have definite ideas and thoughts on these subjects. Write what you want regarding these subjects. Someone else may benefit from your words of wisdom!

The section on Family and Family Background will differ for individuals who are adopted or who are adoptive parents. You may not have any particulars about birth parents but a wealth of information about your adoptive parents. If you are in a single-parent family or a same-sex relationship, your experiences are valuable to others. Your family may have been a warm and loving family, or your family may have been totally dysfunctional. Write from your experience. You may have gained great insight and wisdom of what you think about family dynamics.

Don't hold back just because the questions don't specifically meet your personal criteria. Respond only to the questions upon which you want to reflect, and do not hesitate to make comments of your own that are not included.

There are memory joggers to help you recall events during certain stages of your life. Answer only those that you deem appropriate. Skip the others. Later, you may find that you want to go back and answer more of the questions or address other issues. This is your story. The questions are only there to stimulate your memory and assist you in relating what has been important to you.

Keep a notebook and pen close by at all times so that when a memory pops into your mind, you can write it down and address it later.

Just a word, phrase, name or location should be sufficient to trigger the entry. You may want to start a card file for thoughts, names, pictures, and letters that you want to include but don't have time to write about as they come to your mind. You can also use this card file to ask others to add to the memories mentioned on the card.

You may want to do this process privately or have someone listen as you share the memories. You may want to handwrite your review or to record it on audio or videotape, or you can incorporate all three. You may want to accompany your story with a scrapbook. You may opt to scan pictures into your written text.

Tell family and friends what you are doing. You may need their input with dates, times, names, and places. Use photographs, newspapers, and history references to recall what was happening nationally and locally in political and daily life at the time. Remember that others might remember things differently. That is okay. Do not let differences in recollection cause a disturbance. Everyone sees events from their own perspectives, and that also adds flavor to the stories. You might have to collaborate on dates and locations, but perceptions will always differ.

Don't be afraid to seek help if you find yourself dealing with memories that send you into a tailspin of emotion. This is one reason why having someone assist you in the process might be helpful. Keep the Kleenex handy. You will need it to wipe away tears of laughter as well as sorrow. If at any time along *The Journey* you feel the need for professional counseling, do not hesitate to contact a professional therapist or counselor.

If you are living with a terminal illness, you are encouraged to find someone to help you with this journey of life review. Father J. Mahoney described such a person in his poem.

Wanted

A strong, deep person,
Wise enough to allow me to grieve in the depth of who I am
strong enough to hear my pain without turning away.
I need someone
not too close, because then you couldn't help me to see,
not too objective, because then you might not care,
not too aloof, because then you couldn't hug me,
not too caring, because then I'd be tempted to let you live my life for me.

I need someone
who believes that the sun will rise again, but who does not fear my
darkness or my walk through the night.
Someone who can point out the rocks in my way without making me
a child by carrying me.
Someone who can stand in thunder, and watch the lightening,
and believe in a rainbow.

The journey will be easier with someone sharing and companioning you along the road. Another poem that proved valuable to me was *Companioning* by Dr. Alan Wolfelt, founder and director of the Center for Loss and Life Transition. The center is a private organization dedicated to providing caregivers and others with a greater understanding of individuals who are experiencing grief and loss in their lives. I am grateful for his permission to use this poem

Companioning

Companioning is about honoring the spirit; it is not about focusing on the intellect.

Companioning is about curiosity; it is not about expertise.

Companioning is about learning from others; it is not about teaching them.

Companioning is about walking alongside; it is not about leading or being led.

Companioning is about being still; it is not about frantic movement forward.

Companioning is about discovering the gifts of sacred silence; it is not about filling every painful moment with talk.

Companioning is about listening with the heart; it is not about analyzing with the head.

Companioning is about bearing witness to the struggles of others; it is not about judging or directing those struggles.

Companioning is about being present to another person's pain; it is not about taking away or relieving the pain.

Companioning is about respecting disorder and confusion; it is not about imposing order and logic.

Companioning is about going to the wilderness of the soul with another human being:
it is not about thinking you are responsible for finding the way out.

Once your timeline is completed, you may choose to start your story from the present and incorporate events within the suggested segments. You may want to start with your philosophy of life, your value system, lessons that you have learned and want to share. Next, you may want to share how you want to be remembered. Then you may address experiences at different stages in life that reflect your childhood, education, marriage, and other major life events. Don't forget to complete that list of your favorite things in life. You may want to respond briefly and then return to your writings and really express in detail how you experienced the event you are sharing. Describe what you experienced involving the senses of touch, sight, sound, smell, and taste. Don't just cite a date, time, or place. You may need to do this initially. As you go back, take time to give your story deeper color and emotion. Make it come to life for you and others as you describe what you were experiencing during that particular moment. Write your reactions to the moment then and now. There is a section of reflection with questions requiring deeper introspection. Make sure that you address these issues, especially how you view death and what funeral or burial rituals you want. Many find it a very comforting exercise when it is completed, and the surviving family members' burden is eased because they don't have to second-guess what ritual you would want to use to celebrate your life. This can be a portion of the Ethical Will/Legacy Letter you are going to write. This is the time to share what you want and what you don't want. Be honest and be detailed.

Another component that can be helpful to your heirs is to list those precious items that you want to be given to specific individuals. Take time to tell the story behind the object, the memory it holds for you and for the person to whom you are giving it. The following template is simple to use and can be repeated for each item. You may also want to provide a picture of the item.

ITEM:

DESCRIPTION:

HISTORY OF OBJECT:

PICTURE:

LOCATION:

RECIPIENT:

The Ethical Will/Legacy Letter section is a summary of all you have written previously. Some start in that section and go in the reverse order of the book. Others attempt to answer other sections and progress to the Ethical Will/Legacy Letter portion. Just remember, this is your life, this is your story and you can tell it however you want, in whatever order you want.

Enjoy the process. You will find hope and encouragement along the way, and should you ever need someone to assist you, I am always available. If you should want to share your story with me, I would love to read what you have written. I am just an email, phone call or letter away. I promise to respond quickly.

I wish you peace, joy, love, encouragement, hope and laughter as you spend time celebrating you and your life's journey.

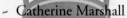

"Often God has to shut a door in our face so that he can subsequently open the door through which He wants us to go."
~ Catherine Marshall

Turning Points

This section was influenced by the works of Dr. Barbara Haight and Jeffery D. Webster in *The Art and Science of Reminiscing* published in 1995. What are those moments in your life where the direction in which you were headed changed their paths? It could have been a major life event such as an illness, the death of a loved one, or meeting that someone you knew you had to marry. It could have been the birth of a child. Many times the words or actions of others can change our life's direction. Words of encouragement might inspire us to tackle goals we might never have attempted on our own efforts. Words of criticism and doubt can cause us to give up and go in a different, perhaps safer, direction, keeping us from achieving our fondest dreams. Sometimes the events are within our control; sometimes they are not, such as the divorce of parents, lost employment, residential changes, accidents or diagnosis of chronic or terminal illnesses. Now is the time on your journey to reflect on the turning points in your life and to see how they affected where you are now. This can be an emotional exercise. I encourage you to be honest with what you write and to try to find some positive aspects of those times. What wisdom did you gain? If it was a horrible experience with no really good ending, how do you let it go? How do you reconcile it and continue your journey with healing and a new found peace-of-mind?

I discovered that I had to forgive certain people for their treatment and their words that affected me so deeply. It was one of the most freeing exercises of my entire journey. I hope you will experience healing and joy as you travel these roads. When you complete this exercise, perhaps you can celebrate where you are now because of where you have been!

HISTORY OF THE MAJOR TURNING POINTS OF YOUR LIFE

Think of your life as a winding road with many detours or side roads. You might think of a large oak tree with many branches or you might envision your life as a flowing river twisting and turning along its course. Turning points are events, experiences, and happenings in our lives that significantly affect the direction or flow of our lives. They are experiences that shape our lives so that, in some important ways, they are not the same as they were before.

What have been the major turning points in your life from your point of view?

What were the events, experiences, and interactions with people and places that have had a major influence or impact on the way your life has flowed?

Dr. Haight and Webster provide guiding, sensitizing questions. You may want to simply write a few words or a phrase and then elaborate on it later. Remember, this can be emotional. As you begin, do not spend all your time on those negative turning points. If we are lucky, most of our turning points have led to wonderful moments in our life that would not have happened otherwise. If you find that you get down and depressed, focus on the positive ones. You may want to combine work on this exercise with some of the humorous events in your life. You can always go back when you have gained a new perspective and refreshed your energies to tackle some of those hard-to-deal-with life events.

"About how old were you when the event/experience happened? Place the turning point along a time dimension. That timing of an event is often very important. In your view, did it happen too soon? Were you too young? Did it happen too late? Were you too old?"

Significant People

Who were the important people involved in the turning point? What was their relationship to you? Were you alone? Often people see that the same people are involved again and again in major life turning points.

Emotions and Feelings

What were the feelings and emotions you experienced at the time the turning point occurred? How intense were these feelings? Sometimes we react to experiences with very mixed emotions. We feel one way one moment and then suddenly feel another. This can be a time of great confusion. Share how you handled those emotions.

EMOTIONS AND FEELINGS NOW:

Sometimes our feelings about an experience or event change over time. People often say that "time heals." What emotions and feelings do you experience as you think about the turning point now? Are they the same emotions you felt at the time of the turning point? Perhaps you have not resolved this issue. You may need to seek help in doing so.

PERSONAL CHOICE:

How much personal choice was involved in this turning point? How much personal control did you have? Was this turning point completely of your choice, or was it something that happened that was totally beyond your control (e.g., flood, parents decided to move the family, divorce, death)? If the turning point was not completely within your control, who or what else influenced the occurrence of this turning point?

CONSEQUENCES:

Turning points are turning points because they change our lives in important ways. In what ways was your life changed or different because of this turning point? What effects, impact, or consequences did this turning point have on your life? Why was this turning point a turning point?

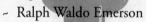

"Every man is a quotation from all his ancestors."
~ Ralph Waldo Emerson

Personal Data

BIRTH INFORMATION

Birth statistics: Length, weight, hair color, etc.

What is your name?

Were you named for anyone? Who? Why was your name chosen?

Where were you born? Name town or city, county, and state.

When were you born? Do you know the name of the hospital?

Who were your parents?

What special circumstances surrounded your birth?

Were you adopted? Share what you know about your birth family/adoptive parents.

CURRENT INFORMATION

What date did you begin *The Journey*?

Why did you begin? What do you hope to gain from this project?

Is someone companioning you along this journey? Share who this person is and how you selected him/her to be with you on *The Journey*.

How old are you now?

How is your health?

Where are you currently residing?

What is your marital status?

Describe yourself emotionally and physically.

"The wise man must remember that while he is a descendant of the past, he is a parent of the future."
~ Herbert Spencer

Family Background

I saw behind me those who had gone
and before me those who are to come,
I looked back and saw my father and his father,
And all our fathers, and in front to see my son,
And his son, and the sons upon sons beyond.
And their eyes were my eyes.
As I felt, so they had felt and were to feel,
As then, so now, as tomorrow and forever.
Then I was not afraid
For I was in a long line that had no Beginning and no
End, and the hand of his father grasped my father's hand and
All up and down the line that stretched from time that was to time
that is and is not yet,
Raised their hands to show the line, and we found that we were one
Born of Woman, Son of Man
Made in the Image,
Fashioned in the womb by the Will of God, The Eternal Father

From "*How Green Was My Valley*" by Richard Llewellyn

"To forget one's ancestors is to be a brook
without a source, a tree without a root."
~ Chinese proverb

Family Tree

My Family Tree

"Wisdom is to be gained only as we stand on the
shoulders of those who have gone before."
~ Learned Hand

Family Heritage

SHARE INFORMATION ABOUT YOUR GREAT-GRANDPARENTS.

What were their names and where were they born?

Maternal Great Grandfather

Maternal Great Grandmother

Paternal Great Grandfather

Paternal Great Grandmother

What stories do you remember hearing about them? Do you recall any family stories or legends about them?

What were their occupations?

TELL ABOUT YOUR GRANDPARENTS.

What were their names?

Maternal Grandfather

Maternal Grandmother

Paternal Grandfather

Paternal Grandmother

Did you know them? What do you remember about them?

Did you have nicknames for them? What were they and why were the nicknamed that?

Do you recall any family stories or legends about them?

What were their occupations?

What were their religious practices?

Describe the special times you spent with them.

Share the lessons they taught you.

How did they influence your life?

Are they still living? If not, how did their deaths affect you?

"Family isn't about whose blood you have.
It is about who you care about."
~ Trey Parker and Matt Stone, South Park , 1999

Family Background: Parents

What is/was your father's name? Describe him.

What is/was your mother's name? Describe her.

Do you have nicknames for them? What are they and why do you call them that nickname?

Are they still living? If not, how did they die? How has their death affected you?

When were they married? Are they still married? Share any stories you might know about their courtship and wedding.

What are your happiest memories of your father?

What are your happiest memories of your mother?

Share any painful memories of your father.

Share any painful memories of your mother.

Share some funny moments you remember about your parents.

What are the lessons and values of life they taught you?

What are some of the family traditions you had? Have you continued them?

How did you celebrate holidays? What was your favorite holiday and why?

How did your family spend vacations?

What was your most memorable vacation?

If you were adopted, please answer the above questions about your adoptive parents.

Tell about any aunts and uncles and their relationship with your parents and with you.

" I think people that have a brother or sister don't
realize how lucky they are. Sure they fight a lot, but to know
that there's always somebody there, somebody that's family."
~ Trey Parker and Matt Stone South Park, 1998

Family Background: Siblings

What are the names of your brothers? Give their dates of birth or birth order.

What are the names of your sisters? Give their dates of birth or birth order.

What were their nicknames?

Who were you the closest to and why?

Describe your relationship with each sibling during childhood.

Are they still living? What is your relationship now?

Where are they currently living?

How often and how do you spend time with them?

How many children do they have? Tell about them.

If they have died, at what age did they die and how did their death affect you?

How did they influence your life?

What lessons did they teach you?

Share some of the most cherished memories you have of your siblings.

What are some of the funny moments you shared with your siblings?

"Most of what I really need to know about how to live and
what to do and how to be, I learned in Kindergarten."
~ Robert Fulgrum

Childhood

What is your earliest childhood memory?

Describe yourself as a child.

Was your childhood happy or sad? Explain.

Tell about any pets you might have had.

What do you remember about the town where you lived? Where was your favorite place to go?

Describe the scenery, special places, and monuments.

What was your family's economic status?

What were your parents' occupations?

What role did religion play in your family life?

What church or place of worship did you attend?

Tell about the special moments you experienced in church or place of worship.

Draw a floor plan of your childhood home (reference example in Table 2). What memories does this bring to you?

When, where, and how long did you live in this home?

What was your favorite room in the house and why?

Describe your secret place if you had one.

What was the yard like? Did you have room to play?

What were your neighbors like? Who were your favorite/least favorite neighbors and why?

Who were your favorite playmates?

Who was the neighborhood bully?

Share your memories about moving and/or leaving home.

How did your family spend their leisure times?

What were the house rules, family standards and expectations of you as a child?

Share your happiest childhood memory.

Share your most painful childhood memory.

How did you spend the summer?

What was Christmas morning like?

What chores did you and your siblings have?

What childhood illnesses and accidents do you remember?

Who taught you to ride a bike, skate, sew, cook, play sports, or fish?

What was your favorite sport to play and/or to watch?

What were your hobbies?

Describe any special collections you had?

Who were your heroes and why?

What is the funniest thing you remember about your childhood?

What were lessons you learned as a child that helped you in later years?

It is the mark of an educated mind to be able to
entertain a thought without accepting it.
~ Aristotle (384 B.C.- 322 B.C.)

Only the educated are free.
~ Epictetus (55 A.D.-135 A.D.)

Education's purpose is to replace an empty mind with an open one
~ Malcom Forbes

School Days

What are your earliest memories of school?

What schools did you attend?

Where were they? Were your schools public or private schools?

What was your transportation to and from school?

Who were your favorite teachers? Why?

Who were some of your classmates?

What did you like most/least about school?

What were your favorite subjects and why?

What kind of student were you? What were your family's expectations of you as a student?

Who was a mentor for you?

Who was your rival? Why?

What were your extra curricular activities? Were you a member of any clubs and organizations? Which ones? Did you serve as an officer or chairman?

Did you and your friends have a special place to hang out after school? Describe what it was like and what you did.

What awards or recognitions did you receive?

Did you graduate? What year?

How did you feel your schooling prepared you for your adult life?

What was your most memorable event in school?

What was your least memorable event in school?

"You cannot have youth and the knowledge of it at the
same time. For Youth is too busy living to know and
knowledge is too busy seeking itself to live."
~ Kahil Gibran

"My parents taught me that I could do anything I wanted
and I have always believed it to be true . . . add a clear idea of
what inspires you, dedicate your energies to its pursuit and
there is no knowing what you can achieve. Particularly if
others are inspired by your dreams and offer their help."
~ Pete Goss

Teen Years

Describe yourself as a teenager.

Describe your family life during these years.

Describe your relationship with your parents.

Describe your relationship with your siblings.

What responsibilities did you have as a teenager?

What part-time/summer jobs did you have? Which was your favorite and why?

How did you spend your earnings?

Who were your friends?

With whom do you currently keep in touch?

Who were your high school sweethearts?

Describe that first date, first kiss.

What adults influenced your life the most and how?

What was the hardest obstacle you had to overcome as a teenager?

How did you overcome that obstacle?

What role did religion play in your teen years? What place of worship did you attend?

What religious questions did you have?

What were your beliefs about God and your role in the universe?

Were there any world events that impacted your life?

How did you share your faith?

What were your beliefs and standards of right and wrong?

What impact did your peers have on your behavior and thinking?

What were your attitudes toward, sex, smoking, drugs and alcohol?

What were the fads of the time? Did you have a favorite fad?

What were some of the slang expressions during these years?

What music was popular and who was your favorite musician?

What movies do you remember? What was your favorite?

What was your favorite book?

What were your hobbies and leisure time activities?

What was your funniest memory?

What was your happiest memory?

What was your saddest memory?

What was your most embarrassing moment as a teenager?

What was your greatest fear?

Did you overcome it and how?

Whom did you turn to for advice?

What advice did they give you?

Who did you most admire and why?

What were your greatest accomplishments as a teen?

What were your greatest failures as a teen?

Would you do things differently or did you learn from these failures?

What else would you like to share about your teen years?

What type of memorabilia do you still have from your teenage years?

"The direction in which education starts a
man will determine his future life."
~ Plato (427 B.C. - 347 B.C.)

Additional Education

Where and when did you attend, college, trade or professional school?

Why did you select this institution?

Why was it important for you to continue your education?

Who encouraged you? How?

Describe the admission process. Do you remember the essay you had to write?

What was your major and why did you select it?

How did your major affect your profession as an adult?

Describe yourself as a student academically and socially.

Were you a serious student or did you play too much?

What was your favorite course/teacher/advisor and why?

Did you join a fraternity or sorority? Which one and why? Describe the process of pledging and becoming an active member. Who was your big brother/sister? How did Greek life influence your life as a student and as an adult?

Why did you not join a fraternity or sorority?

In what other organizations and activities did you participate?

What jobs did you have on-campus/off-campus?

What honors and awards did you receive?

What role did your parents play in your higher education?

What was your relationship with parents/siblings during this time?

How did college or tech school or professional training change you intellectually, emotionally, physically, etc.?

Did you make the most of this additional education? Why or why not?

How were you exposed to diversity?

Did you experience prejudice based on gender, race or religion? How? What was your reaction?

What was the funniest moment during college that you remember?

What was the most memorable event?

What were the happiest memories?

What were the saddest memories?

Have you attended any reunions and what did you think about them?

With whom do you still remain in contact?

How did college help you later in jobs, life, and family?

Is there anything else you want to share?

"God made Truth with many doors to
welcome every believer who knocks on them."
~ Kahil Gibran

Religion and Spirituality

How has religion or spirituality been important to you? How did your religious beliefs affect your life?

What religion do/did you practice? How did you practice your religion?

At what age did religion become important to you? Do you remember the moment when you first believed? Please share that moment.

How did your belief system change over the years?

What church, synagogue or temple do you attend now?

Who has been the most important spiritual or religious leader in your life? Why?

What is your favorite hymn?

What is your favorite scripture?

What is your favorite prayer?

What is the most meaningful spiritual experience you have had?

What are some spiritual lessons you want to share?

"Let every nation know, whether it wishes us well or ill, that
we shall pay any price, bear any burden, meet any hardship,
support any friend, oppose any foe to assure the
survival and the success of Liberty."
~ John F. Kennedy 1961 Inaugural Address

Military

What branch of the military did you serve? How long did you serve?

Where did you serve?

Did you serve during a time of war? Were you in combat? Describe your experiences.

Did you receive any medals or decorations? What were they for?

Describe your family situation at the time of service.

Who were your friends? Do you still keep in touch with them?

Who was your favorite/least favorite superior? Why?

What were your favorite memories?

What were your most painful memories?

What else would you like to share about military life?

If any of your fellow soldiers died, what affect did it have on you?

Who were you related to that was serving in the military?

When was this and where were you living?

What changes in your everyday life were experienced?

What were your feelings then and now about war and military service?

"Choose a job you love and you will never
have to work a day in your life."
~ Confucius

"The road to happiness lies in two simple principles; find
what it is that interests you and that you can do well, and
when you find it, put your whole soul into it . . . every bit
of energy and ambition and natural ability you have."
~ John D. Rockefeller III

Careers

What was your first job that allowed you to be self-supporting and independent? When was this and where?

How long did you work there? Why did you leave?

Did your education influence your choice of careers? How?

What were your career goals and dreams during your first years of independence and work?

Who was your first boss? What did you think of him/her?

What did you like the most/least about your first job?

What other jobs did you have?

What has been your most/least favorite job?

Who was your favorite/least favorite boss?

What is your current career? How did you arrive at this job? How long have you been in this career?

What setbacks have you had in your work history? How did you handle them? What did you learn from them?

What advice do you have for others regarding career choices?

What major accomplishments did you have in your careers?

Did you work for financial gain or personal fulfillment?

Who was your mentor?

If you could change careers, what would you do instead? Why?

Were you a full-time homemaker? Why did you choose this over a career outside the home?

What have been the rewards of being a homemaker?

What would you do differently? Would you make the same choice now?

What has been your most difficult challenge as a homemaker?

What influence did your choice of careers have on your family situation?

What else would you like to share about your careers?

"Love, that thing we have great difficulty even describing, is the only truly real and lasting experience of life."
~ Elizabeth Kubler Ross

"That is what marriage really means; helping one another to reach the full status of being persons responsible and autonomous beings who do not run away from life."
~ Paul Tournier.

Love and Marriage

What is your philosophy about love?

What is your philosophy about marriage?

Are you married now?

Who did you marry and how long have you been married?

Describe your spouse.

Why did you marry him or her?

Do you practice an alternative lifestyle? Share who your partner is and why you have chosen him/her. How long have you been together?

Have you been divorced? What caused the divorce and how did it affect you? Share the experience.

If you were divorced, did you remarry? To whom and how long were you married?

Were there stepchildren involved? Tell about them.

Have you lost a spouse through death? What adjustments did you make? Share the experience.

Share memories about dating your spouse. What attracted you? Where did you meet? Who introduced you?

Do/did you have nicknames for each other? How did you arrive at those nicknames or terms of endearment?

What was your first date like?

How long did you date before the proposal? Describe the proposal. How long was it between the proposal and the wedding?

Tell about the wedding.

Did you elope? Tell about the elopement and why you decided to elope.

Was there a honeymoon? Where did you go?

Tell about the in-laws.

Describe the first year of marriage. What adjustments did you have to make?

Where did you live? What was your first residence?

What role did religion play in your courtship and marriage?

How did you celebrate holidays as a couple/family? What was the happiest of your marriage?

What was the saddest time of your marriage?

What is/was the best part of being married?

What is/was the worst part of being married?

What was the most difficult challenge you and your spouse had? How did you meet it?

What held the marriage together and made it stronger?

What weakened your marriage and caused the marriage to fail?

What advice do you have for others about dating and marriage?

If you are a single person, how do you feel about your singleness? What advice do you have to share?

What are the advantages of being married/single?

"In practicing the art of parenthood an ounce of example is worth a ton of preachment. When we set an example of honesty our children will be honest. When we include them with love they will be loving. When we practice tolerance they will be tolerant. When we meet life with laughter they will develop a sense of humor. Our children are watching us live and what we are shouts louder than anything we can say."
~ *The Art of Parenthood*. Wilferd A Peterson

Parenthood

How many children do you have? When were they born or adopted?

Describe yourself as a parent. Were you a married, single, adoptive, or step parent?

What is your philosophy of parenting?

What has been the most enjoyable aspect of being a parent?

What has been the most difficult aspect of being a parent?

How did becoming a parent change your lifestyle?

What roles did you and your spouse play in childcare?

Was anyone else involved in caring for your children? Who were they and what were their responsibilities?

Share specifics of your children's births; dates of birth, birthplaces, unusual circumstances surrounding their births.

What are their names? Were they named for someone and what was that person's relationship to the family?

Did any of them have nicknames and how did they get them?

What were some of the accomplishments of your children?

What were some of your children's special talents?

What role did religion play in your parenting?

How did you celebrate birthdays, holidays and vacations?

Did you and your spouse agree on your parenting style? Why or Why not? Describe that style.

How old are your children now? Where are they currently living?

Tell about their marriages, children, and other life experiences.

What are their careers and lifestyles?

Tell about your grandchildren. How do you feel about being a grandparent?

Is your role as a grandparent different from your role as a parent? How?

What were your proudest moments as a parent?

What is the most difficult/rewarding part of being a parent?

Do you have stepchildren? Tell how many and give some specifics about them.

What was the most difficult/rewarding part of being a stepparent?

Are you a single parent? Please share your thoughts on the most difficult/ rewarding part of being a single parent.

Have you experienced the empty nest? Share your experience.

What lessons have you learned from your children?

What would you do differently in raising your children?

What advice do you have for parents?

"I don't want to get to the end of my life and find that I have just lived the length of it. I want to have lived the width of it as well.
~ Diane Ackerman

Middle Years
During the ages of 40–65:

What were the most important lessons you had learned about life by the time you reached middle age?

What losses and transitions have you experienced?

How did you reconcile these into your present life?

What was the best/worst time and why?

Did you change your lifestyle during these years? How and why?

Did you make career changes? What were they? And why did you make them?

Did you retire? When?

What were your feelings when you discovered you were "middle aged?"

How do/did you spend your leisure time? Tell about your hobbies.

Share your involvement in volunteer work or politics.

How did your values, goals, and priorities change?

The Journey

What has been your greatest accomplishment during these years?

During these years did you lose family members or friends to death? How have these losses affected your life?

What effects have your personal beliefs, spiritual experiences and religious standards had on your career, marriage, parenting, coping with tragedy, etc.?

What else would you like to share about the middle years?

~ 129 ~

"People grow old only by deserting their ideals. Years may wrinkle the skin, but to give up interest wrinkles the soul. You are as young as your faith, as old as your doubt; as young as your self-confidence, as old as your fear; as young as your hope, as old as your despair. In the central place of every heart there is a recording chamber. So long as it receives messages of beauty, hope, cheer and courage you are young. When you heart is covered with the snows of pessimism and the ice of cynicism, then and then only, are you grown old, and then indeed as the ballad says, you just fade away.

~ Douglas McArthur

A Time for Retrospection
Age 65 and more

Do you feel that your golden years have brought you freedom or increased burdens?

Explain or describe the events that make you feel this way.

Describe your feelings about growing older.

How do you spend your time? Do you wish you had more or fewer responsibilities?

Who are your friends? How do you spend your time together?

Lee Q. Miller

Describe your relationships with family members. What would you change?

Where are your children/grandchildren living?

Have you changed your residence? Where do you currently live?

How has your standard of living changed?

What type of volunteer or civic work do you do?

Share a specific bit of wisdom that you have attained through your lifetime.

~ 132 ~

What are some of the funniest things that have happened to you as a senior citizen?

What have been the best times during your golden years?

What have been the worst times during your golden years?

How is your mental/physical health?

Have you lost loved ones to death? How has that affected your perceptions about death?

Have you made a will? Do you have a living will in place? Place copies here.

What have you shared with family members about what you want your funeral ritual to be?

What are some of the prized possessions you have that you want to leave certain people when you die? What are the stories associated with these items? Use the template to keep track of your items

ITEM:

DESCRIPTION:

HISTORY OF OBJECT:

PICTURE:

LOCATION:

RECIPIENT:

Describe your experiences of discrimination (age, race, gender, or physical disability).

What misperceptions do you feel society has about older adults? Do you fit any of these misconceptions? How are you different?

"Life is no brief candle to me. It is a sort of splendid torch which I have got a hold of for the moment, and I want to make it burn as brightly as possible before handing it on to future generations."
~ George Bernard Shaw

Questions That Need Answers

Share any unresolved issues you might have with other people.

How can you resolve those issues?

What are your worries, fears, and concerns for your future? What resources do you use to help ease these?

What keeps you motivated?

What are your regrets?

What would you do differently?

Discuss your beliefs, values, standards, religious convictions and feelings about your life as it has progressed. How have they changed?

Evaluate and relate the most important ideas you have accepted in life.

What have you enjoyed most about life?

What have you enjoyed least about life?

What have been the funniest moments in your life?

What have been the saddest moments in your life?

What achievements have brought you the most satisfaction and pride?

Do you feel you have been successful? How and why?

What would you do that you never had the chance to do?

Describe yourself as you see yourself today. How have you changed over the years?

What were life's hardest lessons?

What were the most pleasant lessons you learned about:
Living successfully

Marriage

Finding happiness

Children

Grandchildren

Parents

Siblings

What suggestions do you have for future generations regarding the following:

Civic responsibility

Religion and spirituality

Choosing careers

Health issues

Retirement

Death and dying

Prejudices

Fears

Risks

Humor

Joys

Triumphs

Living successfully

How would you like to be remembered? As a person who . . .

What was your biggest challenge in life?

What was the most important date in your life and why?

Who is the one person who has meant the most to you and why?

If you had all the time in the world, what would you do?

Was there a turn in the road you wish you had not taken? Describe it.

What was a talent you never used? Why?

What do you want as an epitaph?

What is the nicest thing anyone ever did for you or you did for someone else?

What was the most important decision you ever had to make and did you make the right decision? How did you make the decision?

Is there one particular event that changed your life forever? What was it and how did it change your life?

Have you ever survived a natural disaster? Explain.

Have you ever had a close brush with death?

What spiritual experiences affected your life?

If you are dealing with a chronic or terminal illness, how has it changed your life? How do you deal with this on a daily basis?

Have your moments of happiness outweighed your moments of sadness?

If you hold a fundamental truth, what is it?

What is the wisest decision you ever made?

What is something you know now that you wish you had known earlier?

If there are special issues you feel strongly about or recollections or experiences that you have not shared elsewhere, now is the time to share them.

Perhaps there are special messages you want to send. Write them here.

If there have been misconceptions about who you are or what you have done, now is the time to write them.

Is there something you have always kept to yourself that you finally want to share? Please do so now.

Perhaps there are some family secrets that need to be told. Now is the time to reveal them.

What are the most important life lessons that you want to share with future generations?

These are a few of my favorite things…

Favorites

Tell what and why about your favorite things in life.

Book/Author

Song/Singer/Type of Music

Movie/Actor

Color

Food/Snack Food/Recipe

Gift

Flower

Lee Q. Miller

Holiday/ Vacation Spot

Joke

Sports Team

Television Program

Perfume

Season

Leisure Activity/Hobby

Spiritual Leader

Political Leader

Hero

Artist

Quote

Family Tradition

Teacher

Mentor

Topic of Discussion

Politics

Describe the world of Politics during your lifetime

Who were the major political leaders?

Did you ever run and serve in political office? If so describe.

What political party did you belong to and why?

What advice do you have for future generations regarding politics?

Inventions and Technology

How has the technology changed world during your life time?

How did you learn to use this new technology?

What have been the major inventions during your life time?

What impact did they have on your life?

Did you ever invent something or wish you had? Tell about it.

WORLD EVENTS

What world events have occurred in your lifetime?

Describe what impact they had on your life?

Photos

Make sure to gather pictures and sort them accordingly. These will be wonderful memory triggers. You may want to separate them by decades or events and scan them onto your computer so that you can incorporate them into your text.

You may want to contact family and friends if you are searching for that perfect picture that relates to a special event or person.

Writing the story behind the picture is so important. Make the time to place documentation on a sticky note on the back of the photograph. As you organize them into the text, you can write a brief caption. Another suggestion is to start a scrapbook as you find these photos and place them in the scrapbook for safe keeping.

Gathering the photos is one of the most enjoyable times of writing your life story. Memories come flooding back as you hold the picture of your newborn or the wedding picture of your parents. These photos will be the impetus for the sharing and reliving of many stories.

Poems and Meditations

I have found many poems, scriptures and meditations that have inspired my writing. It has been enjoyable for my family to read some of these and to make the connection with my life. I encourage you to make time to place poems, meditations and quotes in your book.

Printing, Binding and Publishing

You will need to do some research of your local print shops for the best pricing of printing your book. Most printers prefer it to be electronically submitted. The most popular office supply stores have the capability of printing and binding your book for you. There are private printers and binders that you can locate on the internet. Make sure you investigate the businesses thoroughly. Conduct some comparison shopping before securing services. There are a great variety of options. Make sure to find the one that fits your needs for the number of copies and distribution opportunities. Please contact me if you need assistance.

"The stories that we tell ourselves function to order our world, serving both a foundation upon which each of us constructs our sense of reality and filter through which we process each event that confronts us every day. The values that we cherish and wish to preserve, the behavior that we wish to censure, the tears and dread that we can barely confess in ordinary language, the aspirations and goals that we most dearly prize—all of these things are encoded in the stories that each culture invents and preserves for the next generation, stories that, in effect, we live by and through."

~ Henry Louis Gates
Literary Critic, Scholar, Writer and Teacher
Chair: African American Studies at Harvard University.

Ethical Will/Legacy Letter

This final section of the guidebook is one of the most meaningful exercises you will complete. I hope the creation of this document will bring you and your loved ones the opportunity to share and celebrate the essence of you. I have placed my personal Ethical Will/Legacy Letter at the close of this book as an inspiration for you to create a document that is uniquely you.

Wills have changed over the centuries. Earlier wills expressed a testator's spiritual beliefs, burial instructions and special blessings as well as who were the heirs of the estate. Today's wills focus mainly on the disposition of the deceased's estate and rarely mention spiritual values and beliefs. Here is the opportunity for you to prepare a document that summarizes many of the sections you completed in *The Journey: A Celebration of Life*. This section will guide you in the process of writing your Ethical Will/Legacy Letter that will serve as a legacy for your future generations.

What is an Ethical Will/Legacy Letter? It is a document that reflects the writer's values and beliefs. The document may include spiritual values, hopes for future generations, expressions of love and forgiveness. "It is the voice of the heart," says Dr. Barry K. Baines, a physician specializing in hospice care and who is devoted to popularizing this important personal legacy document. Joella Werlin, founder of Familore, elaborates in an April 2003 Oregon Estate Planning and Administration Section Newsletter; "Legacy planning is the spiritual dimension of estate planning, taking measures to ensure that one's values and heritage will be preserved for future generations."

Who should write an Ethical Will/Legacy Letter? Everyone who cares about another person should take the time to put into writing his or her values and beliefs. Engaged couples, expectant parents and grandparents, adoptive parents, teenagers and elders can all benefit from this process. It is not just for someone facing terminal illness or for those in the later years of their lives. It is an opportunity for others to know who you are and to be remembered the way you want to be remembered.

In my research of over 200 wills between the years of 1770 and 1993, there were numerous commonalities to be found in the older wills and testaments. Along with designating the heirs of the possessions of the testators, religious and spiritual testimonies were often given that included the individual's personal and spiritual beliefs and values. Burial instructions were also given, and often expectations of behavior of the heirs determined the extent of those inheritances. Individuals could rule from the grave. Baines and others caution that the ethical wills should not dredge up family skeletons or put individuals on guilt trips. It is to be an uplifting, healing and loving sharing of one's values, beliefs and other personal insights for his or her descendents.

The Ethical Will/Legacy Letter of today is a separate document that can be attached to the legal will. It is not a legal binding document, but can be placed with the legal will for safe keeping. This sharing of personal thoughts and feelings communicates an individual's hopes and wishes for the future. It provides a clear and true picture of one's values and beliefs. The Ethical Will/Legacy Letter can also include life's lessons on love, faith, forgiveness, education, death and more. It is a time to express gratitude to others for their involvement in one's life. An individual can provide explicit instructions for funeral ritual and burial.

Some people like to share their Ethical Wills/Legacy Letters with their families when they are still living in the hopes of deepening bonds with loved ones through more meaningful discussions. Others prefer to secure the Ethical Will/Legacy Letter with their other wills and have them revealed only upon death. Writing the Ethical Will/Legacy Letter can provide a tremendous growing experience for individuals as they begin to put into writing their values and try to impart wisdom to their heirs.

In a May 2003 Robb Report article entitled *Family: Ethical Will Power,* author Harvey Laney notes the surge of self-reflection since September 11. He quotes Boston psychologist Carol Kauffman: "Ethical

Wills are not for the weak of heart. You have to sit down, think of your life as a finite experience, and try to convey in writing what is most important to you."

In this same 2003 Robb Report article, Laney shares the advice of Denver attorney Tom McMillen. He advises clients who desire to leave family members a personal message to follow a formula that goes by the acronym ACTS. Although ethical wills are personal, heartfelt expressions rather than rigid legal documents, using the formula ACTS can help provide structure and a starting point. A represents the idea of adoration. You can share with your loved one the qualities that you appreciate about them. It is a time to share how those traits have inspired your life. The letter C can provide the opportunity for confession to family and friends of some things you wish you might have done differently—a better parent, more romantic, more available. Some ask for forgiveness for their shortcomings. Providing insight of why you did not do something a certain way or why you did do something a certain way can provide loved ones with a greater understanding of who you really are. The insight can be extremely healing for everyone involved. The letter T provides you with the opportunity to express your thanksgiving for the presence of individuals in your life and how they have helped shaped who you are today. It is a chance to celebrate who you have become and to be able to thank them for their presence on your journey of life. S is for supplication or an offered prayer for your loved ones. It reminds you to write about your hopes, dreams, and wishes for your heirs. It is a reminder to outline the values you have tried to embody in your life and that you hope your descendents will carry with them into the future.

The following suggestions can help you create a document that will be treasured by your family long after you are gone.

Do not be rash. Experts suggest that you plan your ethical will as carefully as you plan your material will. Take your time, and avoid writing when you are unhappy with a family member. This document will be passed down through several generations, so consider topics that will be of enduring importance.

Reread your ethical will annually. "Our perspectives change," says attorney David Levin. "Sometimes they change internally because of the way we look at life, and sometimes the change is forced upon us because those around us change, sometimes for the good and sometimes for the bad."

Recognize when the time is right: material wills are often written in the face of life-altering events, such as the birth of a child or grandchild, or a health scare. Ethical wills can spring from these same events. One caveat: If your children are very young, your ethical will probably will be a work in progress because you have not seen the people they will become.

Keep it separate from a material will. Experts stress that you do not use an ethical will to make monetary demands upon your heirs. It is permissible to ask that your values be considered (example: "I hope my tradition of supporting the arts will continue"). It is not advisable to require or request money transactions (example: "It is my wish that $250,000 be given annually to the Winthrop Foundation from the family trust"). Because Ethical Wills are not considered to be legal documents, bequeath gifts to a specific charity or organization in your material will.

This exercise is an emotional process. When I sat down to write mine, it took me over a week to write a rough draft. The impact on my emotions was sometimes so powerful that I had to put it aside and just reflect on what I had written. For the first time, I put into writing my feelings for my loved ones and acknowledged the importance of their presence in my life. Often I would say how lucky I was to have my husband and my children. As I wrote exactly what they meant to me and how they had impacted my life, I realized what an awesome family I have. I needed to let them know that many years ago. I will share this with them now, and as their lives and mine continue to change, I will update it accordingly. This experience was of great encouragement for me. The knowledge that who I am and what I value in life will be heard and recognized and carried forth brought a feeling of hope for the future generations of my family. Hopefully, this Ethical Will/Legacy Letter provided a better glimpse of how I see myself and how I hope to be remembered. I pray that as you write yours, you will experience the same emotions of encouragement, hope, love and peace!

To get you started I have provided a shortened version, or a template, that you may use to guide your writing. This should be your document, reflecting the values and beliefs that you want to share with future generations. You may simply want to create your own outline that expresses your beliefs and opinions, how they were exhibited in your lifetime and what knowledge you gained. Should you need the assistance of a professional, I am available.

Following is another example you can use to guide you in the writing process.

Ethical will of _____

_____

Date:

This ethical will is a record of my values and beliefs. I will share a statement of my spiritual faith, the lessons I have learned during my lifetime, and my desires for the future generations. It is a document of hope and blessings, of forgiveness and shared wisdom and love.

I, _____ , believe in:

The lessons I have learned through my life experiences are many. I hope you will gain insight and wisdom from them as you experience similar situations in your individual lives.

Lessons on Love

Lessons on Faith

Lessons on Forgiveness

Lessons on Education

Lessons on Death

Lessons on Life

Statements of Truth:

My hopes and dreams for your future:

Words of gratitude:

I thank you for _____

_____

Words of forgiveness

I forgive you for _____

_____

I request that you forgive me for _____

_____

Funeral ritual for celebrating my life:

Conclusion

Another important aspect of the Ethical Will/Legacy Letter is that it is meant to be shared. If shared immediately with family and loved ones, it can bring about new understandings, deeper appreciations and an abundance of laughter and tears that will heal as well as inspire.

If you would like more information on Ethical Wills, I suggest you do an Internet online search. Barry Baines continues to provide up-to-date information and encouragement for individuals seeking to undertake this process. You will discover numerous explanations and examples of Ethical Wills. Dr. Baines states that, "your Ethical Will is unique because it is shaped by your life experiences that are uniquely yours." This is a major aspect of your *Journey*. It is a summation of the essence of you. My prayer is that this process will be as meaningful to you as it continues to be to my loved ones and me.

The following is the beginning draft of my Ethical Will/Legacy Letter and a poem that resulted from my writings. I have also written a separate letter to my husband and each of my children and grandchild that will accompany the final copy of this Ethical Will/Legacy Letter.

A Simple Celebration

of My Life's Journey

This is my legacy to those individuals whom I have spent time with on my journey called life. I pray it will give to them and to the future generations an idea of my essence and what my hopes are for their lives.

My life's purpose has always been to be an encourager for others. To bring hope, love, joy and peace to anyone in my midst has been my mission in this life. I pray that somehow when you think of me it is with a remembrance of how I might have brightened your day or your life, whether for a moment or for a year or more. Perhaps we shared a laugh or perhaps we cried together—whatever, I pray I was able to share love.

God has been so good by blessing me with so many wonderful people in my life. Thank you for loving me unconditionally, regardless of my shortcomings. I am grateful for the long and wonderful relationships of family and friends. But often times God would also grace my life with strangers—sometimes for only a few minutes, days or months. Some of these people taught me the true meaning of life. They took me outside of my comfort zone and caused me to reach beyond myself as I shared a moment in time with them. They taught me the worth of every individual, and for this I am eternally grateful. They taught me the importance of living in the moment.

There are many life lessons I would like to share with you that I pray you can also embrace. Some you will understand immediately, and others you will have to experience and realize on your own journey. Remember that what I share is shared in love. Take what you can from this epistle to use in your life and to share with others. From this sharing I hope you will come to know and understand more fully the essence of Birdie Lee Quillian Miller, wife, mother, grandmother, mother-in-law, sister, aunt, cousin, and friend.

Embrace your uniqueness.

Challenge your potential.

Be a lifelong learner.

Dance.

Recognize the worth of each individual.

Learn to love unconditionally.

Learn to accept unconditional love from others.

Develop and practice your spirituality.

Put others before self.

Laugh often.

Be a wise risk taker.

Know that you are the only one responsible for your happiness.

Practice forgiveness.

Pray.

Cherish the Earth. It is the only one we have.

Always have a pet.

Plant a garden.

Erase racism from your life.

Maintain your integrity at all times in all circumstances.

Develop a strong work ethic.

Think outside the box.

Do not allow others to limit your imagination/creativity.

Write, keep a journal

Paint a picture, create a soul collage.

Find a way to know who you really are.

Don't let the noise of others' opinions drown out your own inner voice.

Don't be trapped by dogma, which is living with the results of other people's thinking.

Sing even if you can't carry a tune!

Watch a butterfly,

Paint your own rainbows.

Always have a kaleidoscope nearby.

Rejoice in each new day, for no one is promised a tomorrow.

Make each day count for something good.

Celebrate you!

My Prayer for You

May you be free enough to allow your spirit to soar.

May you know the joy of quiet moments and the excitement of knowing your life has touched others and made the world a better place for your being in it. May the sacred and holy moments in your life far outnumber those moments of frivolity and meaninglessness.

When others remember you, may they feel a surge of warmth and a peace deep down in their being that your presence in their lives has touched their souls in a way beyond description.

As you reach the end of your journey and walk through the gate, may you feel a sense of celebration and anticipation for all that lies ahead. The best is yet to be.

Lee Q. Miller

May 26, 2006

The following is a prayer offered by my childhood minister, Dr. Carroll Varner at the First United Methodist Church of Morristown, Tennessee. These are my words at the conclusion of every speech, lecture or workshop. It is a fitting end to this book.

May God think through you and give you noble thoughts.
May God see through you and give you splendid visions.
May God live through you and give you life at its best.
Amen.

References and Works Consulted

Colgin, Mary Louise and Thea Simons van der Ven. *It's Your Story, Pass It On*. Colgin Publishing, Manlius, NY, 1986.

Greene, Bob and D.G. Fulford. *To Our Children's Children: Preserving Family Histories for Generations to Come*. Bantam Doubleday Dell Publishing Group, Inc. New York, NY, 1993.

Gulsvig, Margaret. *More Writes and Visits: 41 Topics to Remember*. BiFolkal Productions, Inc. Madison WI, 1993.

Haight, Barbara and Jeffrey Webster. *The Art and Science of Reminiscing*. Taylor & Francis New York 1995.p166–175.

Hartley, William G. *Preparing a Personal History*. Primer Publications, Salt Lake City, UT, 1976.

Herbst, Laurel H.; Lynn, Joanne; Mermann, Alan C.; Rhymes, Jill. "What do dying patients want and need? Patient Care, February 28, 1995 v29 n4 p27 (10).

Isbell, Lou, "Living with Dying Human Environmental Sciences publication GH6851, October 1, 1987.

Kempthorne, Charliey. *A Complete Guide to Writing Your Family History*, Boynton Cook Publishers, Portsmouth NH, 1996.

Laney, Harvey. *Family: Ethical Will Power*, Robb Report, May 2003.

Ledoux Dennis. *Turning Memories Into Memoirs*. Soleil Press, Libson Falls, ME, 1993.

McMillen, Tom, *Robb Report*, May 2003.

Moyers, Bill and Judith Davidson. *On Our Own Terms, Moyers on Dying in America* Leadership Guide. Public Affairs Television, Thirteen WNET, New York, NY, 2000.

Parkes, Colin Murray, "The dying adult." *British Medical Journal*, April 25, 1998 v316 n7140 p 131 (3).

Pavuk, Pamela and Stephen. *The Story of a Lifetime.* Tri Angel Publishers, Augusta, GA, 1996.

Pelaez, Martha, Ph.D. and Paul Rothman. *A Guide for Recalling and Telling Your Life Story.* Hospice Foundation of America, 1994.

Pengra, Nancy. *Family History.* Family Histories, St. Paul, MN 1995.

Sheridan, Carmel Reminiscence: *Uncovering a Lifetime of Memories.* Elder Books, Forest Knolls, CA 1998.

Internet References

Baines, Barry. www.ethicalwill.com.

Butler Reviews Life Review. Robert N. Butler. "Aging Today The Legacies of Memory: What Elders Bring To The Future." http://www.asaging.org.

"Coping and Hoping: A Collection of Articles for the Bereaved." Hospice and Community Care, Rock Hill, SC.

Strengthening Families and Communities by Sharing Life Stories. Ohio State University Extension Fact Sheet. http://ohioline.osu.edu/hyg-fact.

Kunz, John A. "Giving Voice to Lives: Reminiscence and Life Review." National Council on Aging web site http://www.ncoa.org/publications/innobations/Reminiscence.

Werlin, Joella, familulore.
www.family.org/focusoverfifty/lifewise/a0022207.cfm.

Vyjeyanthi, S. Periyakoil and James Hallenbeck. "Dying and Preparatory Grief," *American Family Physician.* March 1, 2002 v65 i5 p 897.

Vyjeyanthi, S. Periyakoil, James Hallenbeck, "Identifying and Managing Preparatory Grief and Depression at the End of Life," *American Family Physician,* March 1, 2002 v65 i5 p 883.

About the Author

Lee Q. Miller is a personal historian dedicated to enabling individuals to preserve their life stories for future generations to cherish forever. Lee obtained her B.A. degree in sociology and her Master of Liberal Arts degree from Winthrop University, Rock Hill, South Carolina, where she lives with her husband Jerry, their three children and their families.

Lee is published in various academic journals on topics ranging from grandparents raising grandchildren to qualitative research on last wills and testaments covering over 200 years. Her current research is in the areas of aging, gerontology, and current sociological issues. Lee also is a lecturer with the Department of Sociology and Department of Sociology at Winthrop University.

Lee spends her "spare" time facilitating reminiscence and life review workshops for churches, residents in assisted living facilities and community members. Companioning individuals on their *Journey*, public speaking and volunteer training are just a few of the projects with which Lee is involved. Lee has completed the 100 year corporate history of Rock Hill Coca Cola Bottling Company, as well as numerous individual memoirs. She is a member of the Association of Personal Historians.

Lee is ready to assist you on your *Journey* and welcomes your inquiries and responses. If you are interested in workshops, seminars, memoir writing classes, speaking engagements, training or individual sessions, you may contact her at Legacies and Legends, 3147 Wimbledon Lane, Rock Hill, SC 29732, 803–366–3065 or email her at millerjl@rhtc.net.